TICKNER'S CATS

Written and Illustrated by

JOHN TICKNER

The Sportsman's Press
London

Published by *The Sportsman's Press* in 1987

British Library Cataloguing in Publication Data
Tickner, John
Tickner's cats.
1. English wit and humor, Pictorial
2. Cats —— Caricatures and cartoons
I. Title
741.5'942 NC1476

ISBN 9-948253-15-0

Printed and bound in Great Britain at
The Bath Press, Avon

FOREWORD

Whether one is a cat enthusiast, hates cats, or is completely indifferent to cats, it is impossible not to be aware of them. They are individualists and, as individualists, can be seen and heard everywhere, in town and country and in places where no cat should or, one might think, could be.

There were cats, we are told, millions of years before man appeared. This may account for the superior attitude of cats towards men. They were also on earth millions of years before dogs evolved and this, no doubt, has much to do with their condescending manner even towards the dogs they select to treat as part-time companions.

Cats, despite their cosy appearance when sitting on one's lap, sleeping in front of the fire or curled up in one's favourite chair, have one great interest in life – themselves. A cynic might comment that is why cats and humans seem to get on so well. Enthusiastic cat persons would deny it, especially if their own cat appeared to be listening.

Whether one approves of cats or not, there is no denying that they have infiltrated almost all forms of human activity, from domestic to sporting.

Their association with humans is by no means confined to

sentimental females. Men in all walks of life, some of them famous, have been owned by cats and many a keen sportsman has his favourite feline companion, even if he hates the sight of any others of the species. Non-sportsmen might be surprised to learn that there are even tough professional gamekeepers, famed for their loathing of cats in general, who sit behind closed curtains with cats purring on their laps.

There are cats co-habiting with horses in hunting and racing stables, living in cricket pavilions and football establishments and mingling with the directors of many an industrial company.

The cat, it seems, shared life with man as soon as the latter was invented and, so long as there is food and comfort available, always will.

JOHN TICKNER
Westhide,
Hereford.

EARLY CAT

Cats began their association with man at the highest level, training him to regard them as sacred animals right from the start. Man has, therefore, been worshipping cats for centuries and cat has every intention of keeping it that way.

Bronzes of sitting cats were popular in Ancient Egypt and you often see modern cats sitting on your garden wall, pretending to be bronzes in the hope that you will rush out and worship them.

These days only the most ardent cat-worshippers are likely to prostrate themselves before cats but sometimes they can be found doing so, flat on their faces, holding out offerings of milk to persuade the bronzes to come indoors.

CAT PERSONS

Unlike many who are devoted to a specific section of the animal world, cat persons cannot always be identified on sight. With few exceptions, one cannot say "that is a cat person" as one can usually do with horse persons and, to a lesser extent, dog persons.

Cat persons are often heavily disguised anyway. The ignorant may think that all cat persons are little old ladies. Far from it. Many a tough weather-beaten old soldier or sailor or airman is a secret cat fanatic.

Foremost among the favourite subjects for adoption by cats are persons living on their own although a really cunning cat will also take time off visiting other persons who will bribe it to go away.

Artists, writers and clergymen are often enthusiastic cat persons and this is probably due to the solitary home life they lead. Cats are often to be found in the studies of ancient vicarages helping ancient vicars to write their sermons or their nature notes. One of the genuinely good things about cats is their helpfulness and they are particularly good at helping themselves.

There are also many successful family cats who become everybody's favourite by talking to each member of the family alone and convincing them that they are devoted to them only. When the whole family is present it pretends to be an aloof sort of cat in order not to make everyone jealous.

Actors and actresses are immensely popular with cats who can earn an excellent living by appearing at the right moment in a theatre and forecasting a successful run for a play or by making a pet of a leading lady and helping itself to her chocolates and currying favour with her most generous admirers.

Film and television persons are often cat fans and many a furry star has achieved fame by sitting around and going for an occasional stroll across the screen or helping to write actors' memoirs.

Advertising cats have a wonderful time. All they have to do is to jump about a bit and eat something out of a tin and pretend they never eat anything else.

CATS
LOVE
CATTYWINK
CAT FOOD
FROM ALL THE
BEST GROCERS

To the amazement of cats there are in existence non-cat persons who cannot stand cats. This group includes bird-watchers who prefer to bother birds without the assistance of cats, poachers who resent competition, most gamekeepers and all shooting persons who are apt to mistake them for other furry creatures.

Non-cat persons who are genuinely allergic to cats, go all over peculiar whenever a cat comes near and, in extreme cases, run screaming over the horizon. Cats, having a sadistic sense of humour, make a point of paying close attention to this type of person. The victim's reaction gives them a great sense of cat power.

The humans most popular with cats are the stray cat persons and they are especially popular with confidence-trick cats who gang up and pretend they are homeless and foodless.

These crook cats meet regularly and have their headquarters in dense undergrowth or dark cellars in empty houses. They send out patrols to con soft-hearted cat persons into putting out extra rations for them.

Then they go home, grinning all over their faces and pretending they have had a hard day's mouse-hunting, to stuff themselves with whatever regular meal their regular cat person gives them.

THE MIND OF A CAT

Cats, like Oriental humans, are inscrutable. Inscrutable, according to the dictionary, means, "Incapable of being found out by searching or reason" and whoever heard of a cat that was capable of being found out?

As a cat keeps its mind very much to itself, one can only make a guess as to what it is thinking, most of the time, but it is fairly certain that, even when apparently staring at you blankly or rudely, it is thinking about food, comfort or its love-life, in that order. Very often it is thinking about all three.

When its love-life concerns the cat next door the whole district is informed, usually in the middle of the night.

Cats who have given up any interest in love-life because of interfering vets or old age (and they would have to be very old indeed) think a lot about food.

They unashamedly stare at any food out of reach, particularly if you are eating it. If there is no food in sight they stare at where it is kept and think about how to get at it.

Cats have always refused to share the human failing of having a conscience. What's yours is theirs, a cat thinks to itself, and follows the thought to a logical conclusion whenever possible.

Cats may betray what they are thinking by body language, to some extent. A gently waving tail means the cat is pleased about something, not necessarily you; it is more likely it is pleased about some foul cat plot it has just thought up.

A violently-waving tail means the cat is annoyed about something, probably you. A tail held straight out behind means the cat is about to attack, say the experts. If it is expressing itself loudly in cat language at the same time, it means you have shut its tail in the door.

A COUNTRY CAT

Wherever there is any country left, there are country cats. Like country humans, they are rugged individualists and great characters and all that. Like country humans, they are very good at sitting hairily behind pint pots and pretending to be oldest inhabitants, but they are aiming at getting a free meal rather than a free pint.

The country cat has the disadvantage of having to work for its own living, unlike the average town cat. On the other hand, it can sit peacefully on the edge of cornfields waiting for field mice to come out and have picnics. And as long as it avoids motorways it is less likely to be squashed by traffic.

The country cat has the advantage of being free to come and go as it likes. It can stroll out of doors with its paws in its pockets, so to speak, going where it likes, sunning itself on quaint old cottage doorsteps or wandering about farmyards, chatting up cows and pigs and things.

It learns from kittenhood that it is inadvisable to loiter near chicken houses and play with fluffy chicky-wickies in case its intentions are misunderstood. It also learns very quickly not to talk to rough old geese and turkey cocks whose behaviour is apt to be rude and even violent.

TOWN CAT

A high proportion of the cat population became town cats as soon as towns were invented. Cats were comfortable enough living in isolated man-made dwellings, but when civilised men got together, civilised cats got together with them.

Although cats have always been the most hygienic of creatures, it suited them to live with unhygienic man who threw left-over food out of the window and allowed unattended food, such as chickens, to wander about all over the place.

Town cats have always been the boss in the house. If the householder is ever rude to them they can always get their revenge on the furniture and the curtains.

Most town cats retain the cunning of country cats to enable them to do what they want despite human efforts to prevent them.

Although town cats are not usually allowed the complete freedom accorded their rural relatives, most of them seem to find ways of getting in and out of places at will. They have a remarkable ability for going all thin and flat and creeping under and through doors and windows that are scarcely open.

They are also good at curling up and becoming small bumps under cushions and bedclothes and thereby giving humans some horrible shocks.

Town cats can travel for miles without their paws touching the ground. In old towns especially, cats have organised aerial roofways involving fly-overs, over-pussies and under-pussies.

There are also open-air restaurants on flat roofs and, most important, concert platforms. Whereas in the country concerts often have to be held on tool-sheds and garden walls accommodating only small cat choirs, in the towns there are large gently-sloping roofs, as well as extensive flat ones, which will take any amount of massed cat singers.

Cats are even greater snobs than dogs and town cats are the snobbiest of all. They can be seen sitting snobbily at the front door of the best town houses, restaurants and clubs.

The most successful of them make a point of being seen inside the windows looking out. Occasionally they go for a stroll in the gardens in the squares at night and in the best parks.

There is a mutual understanding between pedigree dogs and pedigree cats with the best addresses, to ignore each other and consequently any bad cat- or dog-language you may hear in these superior districts at night, must be made by non-pedigree animals who have strayed into territory beyond their station.

SPORTING CATS

Cats are very sporting but like to organise their own sport without interference from man. On the other hand, they often use his unwitting assistance.

Lurking cunningly in the flower-bed, they observe where the persons of the house throw bits of food to encourage their little feathered friends to nest in the area.

This quaint custom indirectly tends to reduce the dawn chorus and increase the size of the sporting cats who often eat the bits of food as well as the birds.

There is nothing a sporting cat likes better than to go out and roam the woodland rides, sniffing the pure air, and studying the bees and the birds, especially the birds.

The methods used in game-bird stalking are much the same as those employed in garden-bird stalking. The cat lurks in a clump of bracken and bushes and watches where the kind game-keeper is feeding the pheasants daily.

Inexperienced cats sometimes grab a tough old cock pheasant by mistake and become airborne immediately and cats hate flying, except on witches' broomsticks.

Mouse-hunting is not only the official job for which cats are employed but it is also a popular sport with some of them.

One of the reasons for its popularity is that it enables them to be seen legally in areas such as larders and dairies and kitchens and dining rooms which are popular with cats looking for things other than mice.

A cat will argue, quite reasonably, that if, in the course of its legitimate hunting expeditions, it comes across food left carelessly about the place, it is its duty to remove it. Otherwise it might attract vermin.

Dog-teasing is one of the most ancient of cat sports and requires considerable coolness, cunning and iron nerve.

Experienced cats begin by stalking the quarry from the top of a wall. On reaching a spot immediately above the dog, the cat sits down and starts to say rude things about dogs. If there is no immediate reaction the cat steps up the rudery in words and music, running along the wall and repeating the process until the dog is hysterical with rage.

There are many other more subtle methods of dog-stalking but a really clever sporting cat always keeps just out of reach of its quarry, otherwise there would not be any sporting cats about.

CAT BREEDING

To non-cat persons all cats are just cats. Cat persons and cats know that this is far from the truth and that not only are all cats individuals, but there are about 40 recognised species of them.

There are various theories as to how the domestic breeds were evolved from the original wild cats. Most people, and even most cats, don't care but what is remarkable is that even quite ordinary, mild-mannered domestic cats can turn any quite ordinary, mild-mannered domestic human into a wild man even when it does something quite ordinary, like digging in the garden.

Non-cat persons who think there are quite enough cats about, if not too many, will be astonished to learn that there are enthusiasts who encourage the production of more of them.

There are two ways of doing this; one is by letting cats get on with their own affairs and the other is by interfering and arranging a mating.

If you want your cat to get on in the world and move in aristocratic circles, you have to make sure that it mingles with the right cats from kittenhood. Some cats, like some humans, have the most appalling taste in mates.

The planned breeding of pedigree creatures can produce some extraordinary-looking results. In the case of cats they can be quite alarming to non-cat persons.

Cats are bred in many colours and patterns and while a tabby is, to the ignorant, just a cat with stripes and blobs, to the expert it is wearing an organised tabby pattern.

Not only are cats bred in a variety of colours but they are produced to have a wide range of hair lengths, from short and furry, coarse and scratchy, to so long-haired that it is difficult to make out which end is which. Indeed some of them look more like a hat than a cat.

All members of the cat tribe have the ability to find their way across country without maps. Cat persons who have found themselves smothered in cats and have decided to give some of the dear little kittens away, have been deeply embarrassed by this catty talent for returning home across vast distances.

One might think that the way to stop your gift kitten turning up on your doorstep the day after you have given it away, would be to ensure that its new owner gives it plenty of food and comfort as soon as it arrives.

On the contrary, this plan suits some cats admirably; they just commute between the two homes.

CAT SHOWS

Of all animals, cats are the best at showing off. The obvious place at which to earn a high reputation as a cat person is a cat show. Here all the top felines get together and discuss each others' pedigrees and reputations. It helps to be accompanied by a pedigree cat.

There are many cat clubs throughout the world. They hold shows which are organised and attended by cats and cat persons of all colours, shapes and sizes.

It is noticeable that the more successful the competitors become, the more the cats and owners resemble each other. A champion cat and a champion cat person often look almost identical. Some of them sound it, too.

CHAMPION

TRAVELLING CAT

Cats are not usually such good travellers as other domestic animals, except on their own paws. Whereas most dogs and horses, for instance, resign themselves once they have been put into their travelling boxes, many cats object strongly.

They persist in calling out loudly that there is a cat in the basket wanting to get out. Often they underline this with violent action and few things are more disconcerting to travellers in trains and coaches than sitting next to a basket that suddenly begins to howl and jump about.

The odd thing is that the travelling cat always seems to note the route it is travelling and often walks straight back home as soon as the basket is opened.

CAT ANCESTORS

Domestic cats, although they would rather not know about some of their small primitive ancestors, are proud of their grander relatives, such as lions, tigers and leopards. This is indicated by the fact that they tend to imitate the behaviour of annoyed members of the big cat tribes when they themselves are annoyed or frustrated.

The roar of a lion in the African bush or a tiger in the Indian jungle at night is thrilling and romantic. Some domestic cats try to imitate these romantic sounds in one's garden at night.

This is the time to remind the cat that its closer ancestors include the small African Wild Cat, the Indian Spotted Cat and the European Wild Cat. It usually goes away after that.

MODERN CAT

The modern cat is very publicity-minded. Although many of them are still prepared to stay at home, only going out into the gardens to sing at night, there are others who prefer to go out to work daily.

Almost all working cats, apart from professional mouse-hunters, are in the Public Relations business and love to appear in advertisements, especially on T.V.

Cats have many romantic, as well as some sinister, associations. In the bad old days the skins of big cats used to lie decoratively in front of smouldering log fires, particularly in romantic novels. From time to time you can see a tabby cat practising looking like a tiger-skin hearthrug in the hope that it will end up in a novel.

Whatever the breed, type and characteristics of a cat, it will almost certainly eventually gravitate to a cat person's home. You are probably looking at one now.